Jardine

by Iain Gray

GW00994794

Lang**Syne**

PUBLISHING

WRITING *to* REMEMBER

Lang**Syne**

PUBLISHING

WRITING *to* REMEMBER

79 Main Street, Newtongrange,
Midlothian EH22 4NA
Tel: 0131 344 0414   Fax: 0845 075 6085
E-mail: info@lang-syne.co.uk
www.langsyneshop.co.uk

Design by Dorothy Meikle
Printed by Ricoh Print Scotland
© Lang Syne Publishers Ltd 2012

ISBN 978-1-85217-349-4

Jardine

MOTTO:
Beware, I am present.

CREST:
A six-pointed spinning spur,
known as a spurrowel.

TERRITORY:
Dumfriesshire and the Borders.

NAME variations include:

Gairdner	Jarden
Garden	Jardin
Gardiner	Jarding
Gardner	Jardines
Jardane	Jardyne

*The spirit of the clan means
much to thousands of people*

Chapter one:

The origins of the clan system

by Rennie McOwan

The original Scottish clans of the Highlands and the great families of the Lowlands and Borders were gatherings of families, relatives, allies and neighbours for mutual protection against rivals or invaders.

Scotland experienced invasion from the Vikings, the Romans and English armies from the south. The Norman invasion of what is now England also had an influence on land-holding in Scotland. Some of these invaders stayed on and in time became 'Scottish'.

The word clan derives from the Gaelic language term 'clann', meaning children, and it was first used many centuries ago as communities were formed around tribal lands in glens and mountain fastnesses.

The format of clans changed over the centuries, but at its best the chief and his family held the land on behalf of all, like trustees, and the ordinary clansmen and women believed they had a blood relationship with the founder of their clan.

There were two way duties and obligations. An inadequate chief could be deposed and replaced by someone of greater ability.

Clan people had an immense pride in race. Their relationship with the chief was like adult children to a father and they had a real dignity.

The concept of clanship is very old and a more feudal notion of authority gradually crept in.

Pictland, for instance, was divided into seven principalities ruled by feudal leaders who were the strongest and most charismatic leaders of their particular groups.

By the sixth century the 'British' kingdoms of Strathclyde, Lothian and Celtic Dalriada (Argyll) had emerged and Scotland, as one nation, began to take shape in the time of King Kenneth MacAlpin.

Some chiefs claimed descent from ancient kings which may not have been accurate in every case.

By the twelfth and thirteenth centuries the clans and families were more strongly brought under the central control of Scottish monarchs.

Lands were awarded and administered more and more under royal favour, yet the power of the area clan chiefs was still very great.

The long wars to ensure Scotland's

independence against the expansionist ideas of English monarchs extended the influence of some clans and reduced the lands of others.

Those who supported Scotland's greatest king, Robert the Bruce, were awarded the territories of the families who had opposed his claim to the Scottish throne.

In the Scottish Borders country – the notorious Debatable Lands – the great families built up a ferocious reputation for providing warlike men accustomed to raiding into England and occasionally fighting one another.

Chiefs had the power to dispense justice and to confiscate lands and clan warfare produced a society where martial virtues – courage, hardiness, tenacity – were greatly admired.

Gradually the relationship between the clans and the Crown became strained as Scottish monarchs became more orientated to life in the Lowlands and, on occasion, towards England.

The Highland clans spoke a different language, Gaelic, whereas the language of Lowland Scotland and the court was Scots and in more modern times, English.

Highlanders dressed differently, had different

customs, and their wild mountain land sometimes seemed almost foreign to people living in the Lowlands.

It must be emphasised that Gaelic culture was very rich and story-telling, poetry, piping, the clarsach (harp) and other music all flourished and were greatly respected.

Highland culture was different from other parts of Scotland but it was not inferior or less sophisticated.

Central Government, whether in London or Edinburgh, sometimes saw the Gaelic clans as a challenge to their authority and some sent expeditions into the Highlands and west to crush the power of the Lords of the Isles.

Nevertheless, when the eighteenth century Jacobite Risings came along the cause of the Stuarts was mainly supported by Highland clans.

The word Jacobite comes from the Latin for James – Jacobus. The Jacobites wanted to restore the exiled Stuarts to the throne of Britain.

The monarchies of Scotland and England became one in 1603 when King James VI of Scotland (1st of England) gained the English throne after Queen Elizabeth died.

The Union of Parliaments of Scotland and England, the Treaty of Union, took place in 1707.

Some Highland clans, of course, and Lowland families opposed the Jacobites and supported the incoming Hanoverians.

After the Jacobite cause finally went down at Culloden in 1746 a kind of ethnic cleansing took place. The power of the chiefs was curtailed. Tartan and the pipes were banned in law.

Many emigrated, some because they wanted to, some because they were evicted by force. In addition, many Highlanders left for the cities of the south to seek work.

Many of the clan lands became home to sheep and deer shooting estates.

But the warlike traditions of the clans and the great Lowland and Border families lived on, with their descendants fighting bravely for freedom in two world wars.

Remember the men from whence you came, says the Gaelic proverb, and to that could be added the role of many heroic women.

The spirit of the clan, of having roots, whether Highland or Lowland, means much to thousands of people.

*Clan warfare produced a society where courage
and tenacity were greatly admired*

Chapter two:

Divided loyalties

Derived from the Old French 'jardin', indicating a garden or an orchard, the surname of Jardine has numerous variations.

But what they all have in common is that they stem from an original 'Jardine' knight who came from Normandy with William the Conqueror in 1066 and fought at the battle of Hastings.

Those Normans who were granted lands in England, at the expense of the native Anglo-Saxons, later found new territories in Scotland after first being invited to settle there in the twelfth century by the Scottish monarch David I.

Before the form of Jardine became common-place in Scotland, there were often some confusing variations, such as 'de Orchard' recorded in 1296.

Scotland had been thrown into crisis ten years before this date, with the death of Alexander II and the death four years later of his successor, the Maid of Norway, who died while en route to Scotland to take up the crown.

John Balliol was enthroned at Scone as King

of Scots in 1292 – but fatefully for the nation the ambitious Edward I of England had been invited to arbitrate in the bitter dispute over the succession to the throne, and the hapless Balliol was Edward's chosen man.

The Scots rose in revolt against the imperialist designs of the English king in July of 1296 but, living up to his reputation of 'Hammer of the Scots', he brought the entire nation under his subjugation little less than a month later, garrisoning strategic locations.

To reinforce his domination of Scotland, 1,500 earls, bishops and burgesses were required to sign a humiliating treaty of fealty, known as the Ragman Roll, because of the number of ribbons that dangled from the seals of the reluctant signatories.

It is on this document that the name of 'Jordan de Orchard' is found – indicating that by this period the family that would later become better known as the Jardines were judged as being in the higher ranks of Scottish society.

More than a century before this, in 1153, a Wilfredus de Jardine is recorded as having witnessed a charter at Kelso Abbey, and it is reasonable to assume that he was the progenitor, or 'name father', of those Jardines who were settled for centuries in the present day area of Dumfriesshire and the adjoining Borders area.

Twenty-five years later, in 1178, Humphrey de Jardin witnessed a charter at Arbroath Abbey, while a Patrick de Gardines appears on record as chaplain to the Bishop of Glasgow.

It was at Applegirth, on the River Annan, four miles northwest of the present day town of Lockerbie, in Dumfriesshire, that the Jardines had become established by the early years of the fourteenth century, later building their forbidding stronghold of Spedlins Tower.

This remained their seat until the late seventeenth century, until abandoned after the family had been repeatedly tormented by the ghost of a miller whom the Jardine chief had left to starve in the dark and fetid depths of the tower's dungeon.

No longer in Jardine hands, the tower has since been restored from its ruins to once again dominate and grace the surrounding landscape.

Following the abandonment of Spedlins Tower, the Jardines of Applegirth built a new seat near-by – the mansion house of Jardine Hall – but, in common with the tower, it is no longer in family hands.

Honours and titles accrued to the Jardines,

most notably in 1672 when Alexander Jardine of Applegirth was created a Baronet of Nova Scotia.

James VI first granted these baronetcies in 1624 to Scots of substance who were willing to invest in what was Scotland's first attempt to establish a colony in North America. The area for proposed colonisation took in not only present-day Nova Scotia but also New Brunswick and the territory between there and the St Lawrence River.

Nearly forty Scottish magnates, initially, were granted allotments of territory and, although not physically required to take up possession of their distant new lands, a special ceremony was enacted on the Castle Hill of Edinburgh.

It was here that a small area was designated 'Nova Scotia' to allow them to formally take 'possession' of their land and be duly honoured with their baronetcy.

Nova Scotia, in effect, had been 'incorporated' into the Scottish kingdom, while the scheme marked the introduction of the honour of baronet to Scotland.

A combination of factors, including the terms of a peace treaty between England and France, led to the colony finally being abandoned in 1632.

The right to the baronetcy was retained,

however, along with the provision that the title would pass to male heirs, and it is still held to this day by the Jardines of Applegirth.

Another Jardine baronetcy is that of the Buchanan-Jardine Baronetcy of Castle Milk, in the County of Dumfries.

A title in the Baronetage of the United Kingdom, it was created in 1885 for the Liberal politician and businessman Robert Jardine, then head of the powerful company of Jardine and Matheson, of which we will read more in the final chapter.

Representing Dumfriesshire in Parliament, he married the heiress of John Hamilton-Buchanan, Chief of Clan Buchanan, and later assumed the additional surname of Buchanan.

In the English county of Nottingham, there is the Jardine Baronetcy of Nottingham, created in 1919 for the English politician Ernest Jardine, while the Jardine Baronetcy of Godalming, in Surrey, was created in 1916 for John Jardine, Liberal MP for Roxburghshire from 1906 to 1919.

Going back several centuries to the Jardines of Applegirth they, in common with many other families in a time of deeply divided interests and loyalties, opposed the great freedom fighter William

Wallace after he raised the banner of revolt against the English occupation of Scotland in May of 1297.

Proving an expert in the tactics of guerrilla warfare, Wallace and his hardened band of freedom fighters inflicted stunning defeats on the English garrisons, culminating in the liberation of practically all of Scotland following the battle of Stirling Bridge, on September 11, 1297.

This was a battle at which the Jardines fought on the side of the English, as they also did at the battle of Falkirk on July 22 of 1298, when Wallace was defeated.

But, again in common with many other Scottish clans and families, the Jardines later switched allegiance to the great warrior king Robert the Bruce, fighting with honour in his ranks at the decisive victory of Bannockburn in 1314.

At the time of writing, the present Chief of Clan Jardine is Sir Alexander Maule Jardine, described as '12th Baronet and Chief of the Name of the Arms of Jardine and 23rd Chief of Clan Jardine' – and it was this Chief who in the 1970s designed a special Jardine sett, or tartan.

Along with other clans such as those of Armstrong, Bell, Elliot, Graham, Irvine, Johnstone,

Little and Moffat, the Jardines are officially listed with the Court of the Lord Lyon in Edinburgh as one of the clans of the Scottish Borders.

On either side of the border there were three 'marches' or areas of administration, the West, East and Middle Marches, and a record from the late sixteenth century lists the Jardines, along with the Bells, Carruthers, Glendinnings, Grahams, Irvines, Johnstones, Latimers, Littles, Moffats and Thomsons as occupying the West March.

Rightly described by some authorities as Scotland's 'first line of defence' against invading English armies, present day Dumfriesshire and the Borders were for centuries an extremely wild and dangerous place to live.

But it was not only the English that the Border clans had to fear, but also their own neighbours.

This was in the form of reivers, who took their name from their lawless custom of reiving, or raiding, not only their neighbours' livestock, but also that of their neighbours across the border.

The word 'bereaved', for example, indicating to have suffered loss, derives from the original 'reived', meaning to have suffered loss of property.

While the Jardines of Applegirth appear to

have been comparatively law-abiding, they were also not averse from time to time to re-stocking their larders with a spot of reiving at the expense of their neighbours or from across the border.

Chapter three:

Living on the edge

It was in an attempt to bring order to what was known as the wild 'debateable land' on both sides of the border, that Alexander II of Scotland had in 1237 signed the Treaty of York, which for the first time established the Scottish border with England as a line running from the Solway to the Tweed.

This was when the marches were established on either side of the border, with a governor in control of each, at least nominally.

Under this Border Law, complaints from either side of the border were dealt with on Truce Days, when the wardens of the different marches would act as arbitrators.

There was also a law known as the Hot Trod, that granted anyone who had their livestock stolen the right to pursue the thieves and recover their property within a certain time limit.

But this was not enough to curb what had become a state of near anarchy.

In 1603, James VI, after acceding to the throne of England as James I, attempted to solve the problem once and for all by abolishing Border Law and even the very name of 'Borders', in favour of 'Middle Shires.'

But, five years later, matters were still so bad that a Scottish Privy Council report graphically noted how the 'wild incests, adulteries, convocation of the lieges, shooting and wearing of hackbuts, pistols, lances, daily bloodshed, oppression, and disobedience in civil matters, neither are nor has been punished.'

What eventually brought relative peace to the Borders was the settlement in the early years of the seventeenth century of Border clans such as the Jardines in Ireland, in what was known as the Plantation of Ulster.

This was a policy under which they received land grants in Ulster at the expense of what were perceived as rebellious native Irish clans – and it is mainly their descendants who are to be found today in North America after immigrating their from Ireland in later centuries.

In 1573, James VI had confirmed Sir Alexander Jardine in his grants of land at Applegirth and Sibbaldie in Dumfriesshire, Kirkandrews in Kirkcudbright, Hartside and Wandel in Lanarkshire and Jardinfield in Berwickshire.

But this was conditional on that, when required, he would be able to muster at least 240 men to fight for the king.

Nearly fifty years earlier, in 1524, the Jardines had indeed fought for their monarch when, during the interminable Anglo-Scottish Wars, another Sir Alexander Jardine of Applegirth clashed with an advancing English army at Carlisle and took several hundred prisoners – several of whom provided rich ransoms.

But the English repaid this insult 23 years later when Sir Alexander's son, who had succeeded his father as Chief, had his lands sacked by a 5,000-strong invasion force.

In more peaceful times, Sir William Jardine, 7th Baronet of Applegirth, was the pioneering Scottish naturalist who was born in 1800 and died in 1874.

He is recognised as having made a significant contribution to interest in natural history by writing a number of books on the subject, and through his editorship of the 40-volume *The Naturalist's Library*; divided into four main sections, each was prepared by fellow leading naturalists and proved a best-seller throughout the Victorian era.

One footnote on Sir William is that it was not

until 2007, through the BBC television series *Who Do You Think You Are?* that the Olympic Rowing gold medal winner Sir Matthew Pinsett discovered that he is a direct descendant of the naturalist.

Sir William Jardine was also the uncle of the brothers Frank and Alexander Jardine, recognised as pioneering Australian explorers.

Born respectively in 1841 and 1843, the brothers had already been settled on their father's cattle station in Queensland when, in 1864, they embarked on a gruelling 1,200 mile trek from Rockhampton, in Queensland, to Somerset, also in Queensland.

Driving 250 head of cattle and 42 horses, the trip took 10 long months, during which they had to battle the hostile elements.

They arrived in Somerset with only 12 horses and 50 cattle left, and it was here that Frank Jardine settled with his wife, the Samoan Princess Sana Solia, and naming his property "Lockerbie" in fond memory of his Scottish roots.

Both brothers were subsequently elected fellows of the Royal Geographical Society, while the Jardine River, the largest in Australia's Cape Rock Peninsula, is named in Frank Jardine's honour, as is Queensland's Jardine River National Park.

He died in 1919, a year before his brother, who served for many years as Queensland's chief engineer for harbours and rivers.

One leading figure of the great eighteenth century flowering of Scottish literature, art, and scientific and philosophical inquiry known as the Scottish Enlightenment, was the Reverend John Jardine, who was born in 1716 and died in 1766.

A friend and contemporary of such Scots luminaries as the artist Allan Ramsay, philosopher David Hume and economist Adam Smith, Jardine was a co-founder of the influential *Edinburgh Review*.

It was his son, the antiquarian Sir Henry Jardine, who was instrumental along with others who included the novelist Sir Walter Scott, for the re-discovery after more than 160 years of the Honours of Scotland – the sacred regalia of sceptre, crown and sword.

Normally kept secure in Edinburgh Castle, they had been removed for safety to Stirling in 1651 to keep them from the clutches of the occupying forces of Oliver Cromwell.

Following the coronation of Charles II at Scone, a Parliament was held in Perth in June of 1651, and it was decided the Honours should be moved to the more secure Dunnottar Castle, on the northeast coast.

The hereditary keeper of the Honours was Sir William Keith, the Earl Marischall, but he was a prisoner in the Tower of London, and it was his son, John, who managed to successfully convey the Honours to the fortress of Dunnottar.

Held in the name of the Earl Marischall by its governor, Captain George Ogilvie of Barras, it was defended by less than 50 men.

Cromwell's troops set up a siege of the castle, and Captain Ogilvie decided the Honours would have to be moved to a place of greater safety.

Christian Granger, wife of James Granger, the minister of the nearby Kinneff Church, managed to obtain a pass from Colonel Morgan, the captain of the besieging force, to visit Captain Ogilvie's wife.

The sword and scabbard were hidden in bundles of flax and carried by one of the maids out of the castle, while Mrs Granger secreted the crown and sceptre under her clothes: an unsuspecting Captain Morgan even gallantly helped an understandably nervous Mrs Granger to mount her horse.

One other version of the tale is that the Honours were lowered over the cliffs by rope and taken by a young girl who had been gathering seaweed and concealed in her basket.

What is known for certain is that the Honours were hidden for a time in the manse of Kinneff at the foot of the minister's bed.

The crown and sceptre were then hidden under a slab in front of the church's altar, and the sword and scabbard buried under a row of pews.

Dunnottar eventually fell to the besiegers in May of 1652 and was ransacked in a futile search for the Honours.

They were retrieved from Kinneff Church at the time of the Restoration of Charles II in 1660, placed in a large oaken chest, and secreted in a room in Edinburgh Castle and the room sealed.

It was not until 1818, under the direction of Sir Walter Scott and Sir Henry Jardine that the room was unsealed and the precious Honours of Scotland put on permanent public display.

The Honours were joined in 1996 by the equally sacred Stone of Destiny, on which a long succession of Scottish kings had been enthroned, following its ceremonial return after 300 years from Westminster.

Chapter four:

On the world stage

Bearers of the Jardine name have stamped their mark at an international level, through a wide range of pursuits.

In contemporary music, **Al Jardine**, born in 1942 in Lima, Ohio, is one of the founder members of the top-selling American band The Beach Boys. A guitarist and occasional vocalist with the band, he played bass guitar on its first hit single, *Surfin'* released in 1961, while he sang lead vocals on many other hits that include *Help Me, Rhonda*, and *Then I Kissed Her*, while along with fellow band member Brian Wilson he also co-wrote a number of songs.

Inducted into the Rock and Roll Hall of Fame in 1988, he now pursues a successful solo career and plays with the band when the surviving members occasionally reunite for tours.

On the silver screen, **Perla Haney-Jardine**, born in 1997, is the American actress whose film credits include the 2004 *Kill Bill Vol 2*, the 2005 *Dark Water* and the 2009 *Save the Future*, while on the television screen **Stephen Jardine** is a popular

Scottish broadcaster and presenter. Born in 1963 in Dumfries, where his father, the late **Bill Jardine**, was for a time chairman of local football club Queen of the South, he was a co- presenter of the former Scottish Television daily lifestyle programme *The Hour*.

Also from Scotland, **Quintin Jardine** is the internationally best-selling author who was born in 1945 in Motherwell, Lanarkshire.

Turning his back on a career in the legal profession after briefly studying law at Glasgow University, he entered journalism after being taken on as a trainee with his local newspaper, *The Motherwell Times*.

There then followed careers as a government information officer, based in Edinburgh, a political 'spin doctor' for the Conservative Party, and as an independent media relations consultant.

But it was through the success of his first crime novel, *Skinner's Rules*, published in 1993, and featuring the character of Edinburgh policeman Bob Skinner, that he turned to full-time writing.

More than 18 'Skinner' novels have since followed, in addition to another highly successful series of crime novels featuring the character Oz Blackstone.

In the realms of diplomacy, **William Jardine**, born in 1879 in Olida County, Idaho, and who died in

1955, served as the U.S. Ambassador to Egypt from 1930 to 1933 after a term as the United States Secretary of Agriculture, while **Sir Douglas Jardine** was a prominent British colonial administrator.

It was after serving as an administrative officer with the Somaliland Expeditionary Force that, in 1923, he wrote his rather undiplomatically entitled *The Mad Mullah of Somaliland*, based on the Somali rebel leader Mohammed Abdullah Hassan, who had led an armed resistance against Britain, Italian and Ethiopian forces in his country.

Before his death at the age of 58, he had also held the posts of governor of North Borneo, Sierra Leone and the Leeward Islands.

From diplomacy to education, **George Jardine**, born in 1742 and who died in 1827, was the leading Scottish academic who held the professorship of Greek at Glasgow University from 1774 and of logic and rhetoric from 1787 to 1824.

Bearers of the Jardine name have also excelled in the highly competitive world of sport.

In football, **Sandy Jardine** is the former Scottish right-back who was born in Edinburgh in 1948. In addition to playing with Rangers between 1965 and 1982 and with Hearts from 1982 to 1988, he played for the Scottish national team between 1970 and 1979, on nine occasions as its captain, earning himself 38 caps.

Also born in Edinburgh, in 1941, **Fred Jardine** is the former professional football defender who had a distinguished career playing for teams that included Dundee, Luton Town and Torquay United, while **Alex Jardine**, the talented full back who was born in Motherwell in 1926 and died in 1978, played for teams that included Dundee United and Millwall.

In the equally fast-paced game of ice hockey, **Ryan Jardine** is the star Canadian forward who was born in Ottawa in 1980 and who, at the time of writing, plays for Italian team Bolzano-Bozen, while in the boxing ring **Charles Jardine** was the all-round sportsman who took the title of Australian Heavyweight Boxing Champion.

Born in 1889, he was renowned for his skills at rifle shooting, the shot put and throwing the hammer, but it was in the boxing ring that he particularly excelled – winning his heavyweight championship title in 1923. He represented his nation at the Olympics in the following year, but lost out to the boxer and eventual gold medal winner Otto von Porat; he died in 1942.

On the cricket pitch, **Douglas Jardine**, born in Bombay in 1900 to Scottish parents, but playing for the England national cricket team, was the batsman who captained the team between 1931 and 1934.

Nicknamed "The Iron Duke", he is best remembered for his captaincy of the English team during its 1932-33 Ashes tour of Australia, in which the team used controversial 'bodyline' bowling tactics to effectively 'neutralise' the opposing Australian batsmen – particularly the great Australian cricketer Don Bradman. He died in 1958.

In the wrestling ring, **Don Jardine** was the colourful Canadian wrestler born in 1940 in Moncton, New Brunswick, and who died in 2006; among his many ring personas were 'The Spoiler', 'The Butcher' and 'Super Destroyer'.

From the wrestling ring to the American basketball court, **Antonio "Scoop" Jardine**, born in 1988 in Philadelphia, is the star player who, at the time of writing, plays for the Syracuse Orange.

In the rough and tumble that is the game of rugby, **Ian Jardine**, who played for both Stirling County and Glasgow, is the Scottish Rugby Internationalist, born in Dunfermline in 1965, who earned his first cap playing against the All Blacks in 1993.

One particularly enterprising bearer of the Jardine name was **William Jardine** who, from impoverished beginnings, helped to found what thrives today as one of the world's biggest multi-national corporations. One of five children and born in 1784 on a small farm near Lochmaben, in Dumfriesshire, his father died when he was young and it was left to an elder brother to help the financially straitened family.

It was through his brother's help that Jardine was able to study medicine in Edinburgh and, shortly after qualifying in 1802, he joined the maritime service of the East India Company as a ship's surgeon.

Also dabbling in trade, as did most employees of the company, he was able to amass enough money to set up as an independent trader in 1817; by 1832 he had joined forces in Canton, China, with fellow Scots trader James Matheson – and so was born Jardine, Matheson and Company.

The wily merchants traded Chinese tea and silk to Europe while, in return, they traded opium to the Chinese. When the Chinese Emperor attempted to ban the trade in opium and confiscated consignments of the drug, British merchants successfully appealed for help to the British government.

This led in 1840 to what are known as the Opium Wars, as Britain backed its entrepreneurs with armed force against the hapless Chinese.

Jardine and Matheson had also vastly increased their wealth through breaking the monopoly of the East India Company in China – and the families of both men back in Scotland were not forgotten as they regularly sent them money and found positions in the company for their relations.

Jardine himself appears to have been something of a 'workaholic'.

He is reputed to have had only one chair in his office in Canton, and this was solely for his own use: visitors were never invited to sit, and this was in order to impress upon them that he was an extremely busy man with no time for worthless small talk.

He died in 1843, the owner of several properties throughout Britain, including the Lanrick Estate in Perthshire.

The company he co-founded in the early decades of the nineteenth century along with James Matheson survives today as Jardine Matheson Holdings Ltd., although it is more commonly referred to as simply 'Jardines.'

Incorporated in Bermuda and now based in Hong Kong, its vast portfolio of companies includes Jardine Pacific, Jardine Motors Group, Astra International and the Mandarin Oriental Hotel Group.